Super Swimmers

Whales, Dolphins, and Other Mammals of the Sea

Caroline Arnold

Illustrated by Patricia J. Wynne

◠◠◠ Charlesbridge

To the memory of Richard Hewett,
who taught me to see the animal world
through the eye of his camera
—C. A.

For my sister, Mim, who is
pretty super herself
—P. J. W.

gentoo penguin

common cuttlefish

Published by Charlesbridge
85 Main Street
Watertown, MA 02472
(617) 926-0329
www.charlesbridge.com

Library of Congress Cataloging-in-Publication Data
Arnold, Caroline.
  Super swimmers: whales, dolphins, and other mammals of
the sea / Caroline Arnold; illustrated by Patricia J. Wynne.
    p. cm.
  ISBN 978-1-57091-588-8 (reinforced for library use)
  ISBN 978-1-57091-589-5 (softcover)
1. Marine mammals—Juvenile literature. 2. Marine
mammals—Locomotion—Juvenile literature.
I. Wynne, Patricia, ill. II. Title.
QL713.2.A74 2006
599.5—dc22   2005006018

Printed in China
(hc) 10 9 8 7 6 5 4 3 2 1
(sc) 10 9 8 7 6 5 4 3 2 1

Illustrations done in watercolor and ink
Display type set in Elroy and text type set in Adobe Caslon
Color separations by Chroma Graphics, Singapore
Printed and bound by Jade Productions
Production supervision by Brian G. Walker
Designed by Susan Mallory Sherman

ack sea turtle

gray whale

At Home in the Sea

Each summer California gray whales swim in the Bering and Chukchi Seas near the coast of Alaska, eating food that is plentiful there. When fall comes, the whales swim over five thousand miles south to Mexico, where the females give birth to their babies. The young whales know how to swim from the moment they are born. They grow quickly, and by spring they are strong enough to travel with their mothers back to Alaska.

Whales are mammals just like we are. Almost all mammals can swim if they have to, but most live mainly on dry land. Whales and other sea mammals are super swimmers. Their ability to swim enables them to find food, mates, and everything else they need. It helps them to survive in the oceans of the world.

What Is a Mammal?
Animals that give birth to live young and feed their babies milk are called mammals. Most mammals have hair. Whales have only a few whiskers around their mouths.

Other Ocean Swimmers
Marine mammals share the ocean with fish, turtles, seabirds, and other animals.

3

Who Are the Marine Mammals?

Marine mammals live in or near the sea. Their bodies are adapted for life in the water. Each group of marine mammals has its own way of getting around in the ocean.

manatee

dugong

California sea lion

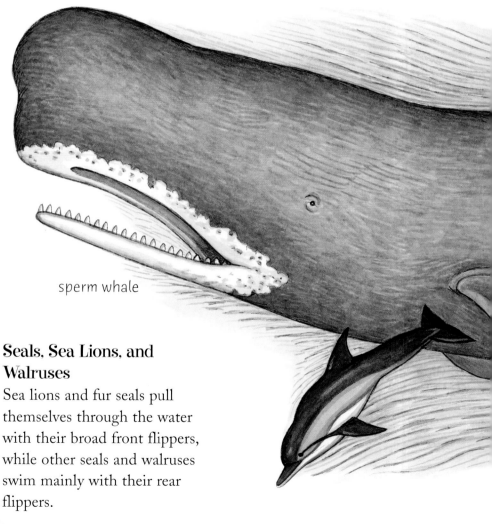

sperm whale

Manatees and Dugongs
These warm-water marine mammals flap their tails when swimming.

walrus

Seals, Sea Lions, and Walruses
Sea lions and fur seals pull themselves through the water with their broad front flippers, while other seals and walruses swim mainly with their rear flippers.

harbor seal

4

sea otters

long-snouted spinner dolphin

Sea Otters

Sea otters paddle with webbed hind feet and use their tails to steer.

Whales, Dolphins, and Porpoises

This group includes the large baleen and toothed whales as well as the smaller dolphins and porpoises. All these animals use their powerful tails to push themselves through the water.

polar bears

Polar Bears

Polar bears are excellent swimmers and are often thought of as marine mammals. When swimming, they use their large, partially webbed front paws to paddle.

5

Bodies Made for Swimming

Most marine mammals are shaped like torpedoes, with small heads and long, round torsos that narrow at the tail. Their limbs are usually short or, in some cases, not there at all. (Whales and dolphins have no hind legs, and their "arms" are their front flippers.) The animals' ears are small; sometimes they are simply holes in their heads. Their skin is mostly bare or covered with sleek fur.

A streamlined body helps a marine mammal slide through the water more easily. Water is more than eight hundred times thicker than air. A swimmer has to push against it to move forward. A smooth outer surface and a curved shape reduce a body's drag, or the pull of the water against it.

Almost all marine mammals have a thick layer of fat called blubber under their skin. Blubber is lighter than water and helps an animal float. It is like a built-in life jacket. Blubber acts like a blanket, keeping the body warm and protecting the inner organs. It is also a reserve energy supply for times when food is hard to find.

beluga whales

torpedo

narwhals

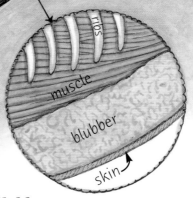

bowhead whale

ribs

muscle

blubber

skin

Blubber

The bowhead whale has blubber up to 18 inches thick to insulate it from the icy water of the Arctic Ocean.

orcas
(killer whales)

Coming Up for Air

Marine mammals breathe air just like other mammals. Air contains oxygen, which they need to live.

Whales, dolphins, and porpoises breathe through an opening called a blowhole in the top of their heads. When the animal dives, its blowhole closes to keep water out. When the animal returns to the surface, it blows air out of its blowhole and makes a misty spout. This spout is the moisture from the breath condensing into a small cloud. The spout for each species of whale has its own shape.

Seals and other sea mammals breathe through their noses. When they submerge, special muscles close their nostrils so water does not get in.

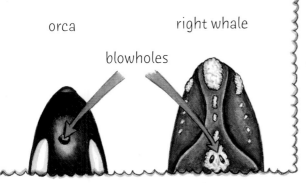

orca right whale

blowholes

Blowholes

The blowholes of baleen whales have two openings. Those of toothed whales, including dolphins and porpoises, have only one.

ringed seals

northern right whale

Breathing Holes

Seals that live in polar regions swim beneath the ice and hunt for fish, using their sensitive whiskers to feel for prey. When they need to breathe, they find a hole in the ice and come up for air. In winter they use the claws on their front flippers to scratch the ice and keep their breathing holes from freezing over.

9

female sperm whale and calf

Sperm Whales

Sperm whales dive thousands of feet deep searching for squid and other food. Whale hunters once caught a sperm whale that had a giant squid in its stomach. The squid was 40 feet long and weighed 440 pounds!

Diving Deep

Most sea mammals come up for air every few minutes when swimming underwater. But some can go much longer without breathing. Weddell seals, which live in the Antarctic, can hold their breath for more than an hour. Sperm whales are also champion divers. They can go more than a mile deep and stay underwater for over two hours. Their bodies are built to withstand the extreme pressure of the ocean depths.

When an animal breathes, air is stored in its lungs. A whale or seal can also store oxygen in its blood and muscles. When a whale or seal dives, its heart slows down and sends blood only to the brain and other organs that need it. That way the animal can make the oxygen last a long time before it has to breathe again.

10

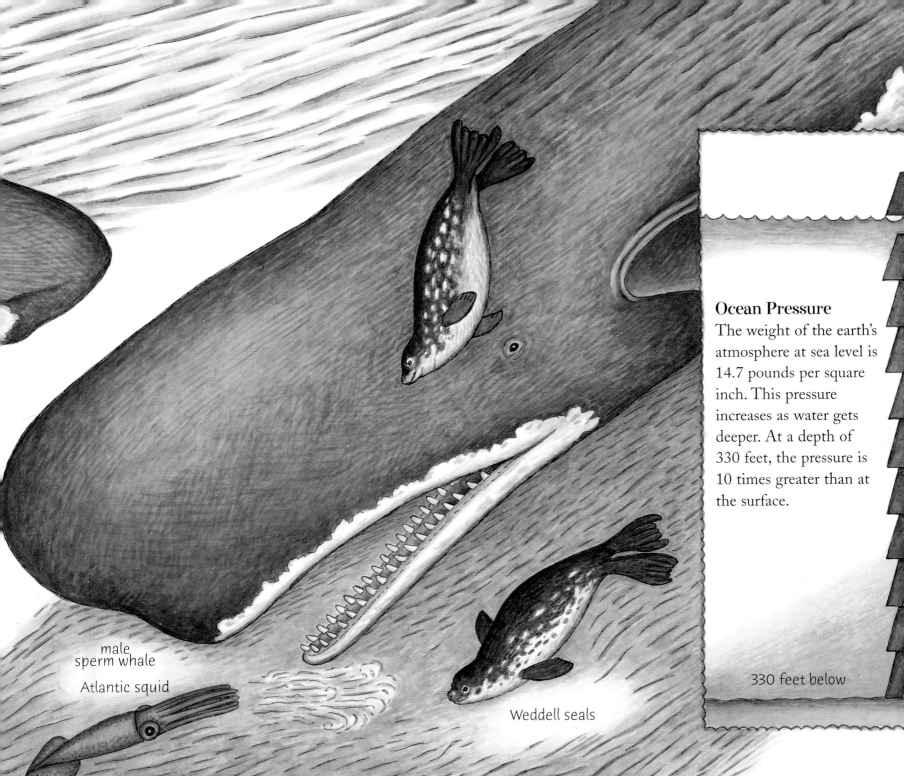

Ocean Pressure

The weight of the earth's atmosphere at sea level is 14.7 pounds per square inch. This pressure increases as water gets deeper. At a depth of 330 feet, the pressure is 10 times greater than at the surface.

14.7

14.7

14.7

14.7

14.7

14.7

14.7

14.7

14.7

14.7

330 feet below

14.7

male
sperm whale

Atlantic squid

Weddell seals

Learning to Swim

Some marine mammals, such as whales and dolphins, give birth to their babies in the water. Others, such as seals, sea lions, and walruses, give birth on land or on ice. All marine mammals are able to swim from the moment they are born. They get better with practice and as their bodies grow stronger.

long-nosed
spinner dolphins

Keeping Up with Mother

A baby dolphin is born underwater, and its mother pushes it up to the surface so it can take its first breath. She will keep her baby by her side until it is strong enough to be on its own. The baby rides in the wave of water, called a slipstream, that its mother makes when she swims. The baby is pulled forward in the wave of water. In this way the young dolphin uses less energy and can keep up with its mother as she moves about.

sea otters

A Free Ride

A baby walrus is usually born on the ice, but it soon goes into the water. The young walrus often rides on its mother's back.

walruses

Belly-Up

A mother sea otter gives birth either in the water or on land, but soon mother and baby spend almost all their time at sea. The baby's fur is so buoyant that the young otter floats like a cork. Most of the time, though, it rides on its mother's belly. It will learn to dive after its sleeker adult fur grows in.

Side by Side

A manatee baby is born in the water. It stays close to its mother, usually swimming behind her front flipper.

manatees

13

plates of baleen

blue whale

Baleen

Baleen is made of keratin, the same material as your fingernails. A whale's mouth can have as many as 400 plates of baleen, each up to 13 feet long.

Baleen Whales

Baleen whales are the largest marine mammals. The blue whale, which can grow to be 110 feet long, is the largest whale of all. This slow swimmer is the biggest animal that has ever lived. Gray, humpback, fin, and right whales are some other kinds of baleen whales.

Whales, Dolphins, and Porpoises

Whales, dolphins, and porpoises are members of the group of aquatic mammals called cetaceans. These animals have broad, flat lobes, called flukes, at the end of their tails. A cetacean propels itself forward by moving its flukes up and down. It steers and balances with the pectoral flippers at the front of its body. Many cetaceans have a stiff dorsal fin on their backs. It keeps the animal from sliding side-to-side as it swims. Cetaceans are divided into two groups: the baleen whales and the toothed whales.

Baleen whales get their name from the long, fringed strips of a hard material called baleen that hang down inside their mouths. As a whale

right whale

humpback whale

fin whale

gray whale

blue whale

peglike whale teeth

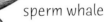
sperm whale

swims, it takes in huge mouthfuls of water and food. Then it pushes the water out with its tongue. The baleen acts like a strainer, trapping food on the inside of the whale's mouth. Baleen whales feed on slow-moving prey, so they do not need to swim fast. The humpback whale, for instance, usually swims at only two to five miles per hour.

The jaws of toothed whales are lined with conical or peg-shaped teeth. Toothed whales are more active swimmers than baleen whales. They chase after fast-moving prey, such as fish, squid, and octopus. An orca can reach speeds of thirty miles per hour when chasing prey.

Toothed Whales

The largest toothed whale is the sperm whale. The male sperm whale averages 55 feet in length. Other toothed whales include the orca, the beluga, the narwhal, and Baird's beaked whale. Dolphins and porpoises are smaller toothed whales, with porpoises being the smallest of all.

sperm whale

Baird's beaked whale

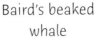

orca

narwhal

common dolphin

beluga whale

15

Speedy Swimmers

Dolphins and porpoises have strong muscles and bullet-shaped bodies that help them speed through the water. Sometimes you can see groups of them leaping out of the waves and then diving back in. This type of swimming is called porpoising.

Dolphins and porpoises can reach bursts of speed of more than forty-five miles per hour. They usually swim five to ten feet below the surface, where there are no waves to slow them down. But they still need to breathe. The easiest and quickest way to get some air is by leaping. As the animals break through the water's surface, they quickly inhale and then dive back down. When porpoising, they can maintain a cruising speed of twenty miles per hour.

common dolphins

Catching a Ride

Dolphins and porpoises are good surfers. They will often swim alongside a boat and use their fins to catch the waves off the boat's bow. The force of the moving water pulls them along.

humpback whales

breaching

spyhopping

clicking noise

echo

bottle-nosed dolphin

Acrobats in the Water

Whales and dolphins are strong and agile swimmers. Sometimes they use their big muscles to jump out of the water. Then they fall back in with a giant splash. This is called breaching. No one knows why they do this. It may be the animal's way of getting parasites off its skin. It may also be a way of communicating with others of its kind.

Sometimes whales or dolphins slap their tails against the surface of the water, making a loud noise. This is called lobtailing. No one knows for sure why they do this either.

Whales, dolphins, and porpoises have good eyesight. Sometimes they "stand up" on their tails and stick their heads straight out of the water. This is called spyhopping. It lets the animal get a good look around.

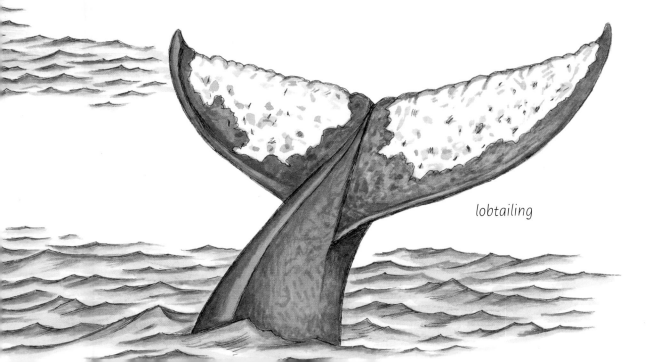

lobtailing

"Seeing" with Sound

Toothed whales make loud clicking noises as they swim. The echoes of these sounds help them detect objects in the water and avoid bumping into them. It also helps the animals find food. This method of "seeing" with sound is called echolocation.

19

Seals, Sea Lions, and Walruses

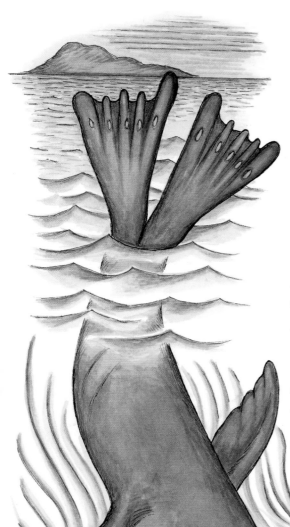

Seals, sea lions, and walruses are adapted for life both in the water and on land. They depend on the ocean for food, but they come to shore to rest and give birth to their pups. There they are safe from ocean predators, such as sharks and killer whales. Although seals, sea lions, and walruses seem awkward on land, they can move surprisingly fast. When on ice, they often slide on their bellies.

Sea lions and fur seals are eared seals. They have a small flap over each ear hole. Their front flippers are large, and they can walk on four limbs. These animals swim by moving their front flippers like oars on a boat. When coming to shore, they often ride the waves like bodysurfers.

Harbor seals, elephant seals, and leopard seals are some of the earless, or "true," seals. They have no ear flaps and their front flippers are small. They swim by moving their rear flippers and lower body in a side-to-side motion. They wiggle like inchworms to move on land.

California sea lions

northern or Steller
sea lion

bearded seal

ribbon seal

harbor seal

21

Tooth Walkers

Walruses live in the Arctic and feed in shallow, coastal areas. These large, tusked animals dive to the bottom and suck up clams, snails, and other food. They may stay submerged for as long as ten minutes, but usually come up to breathe more often than that.

A walrus swims with alternate strokes of its hind flippers and steers or paddles with its front flippers. When a walrus gets out of the water, it may use its long tusks like ice picks to grab hold of an ice shelf or rocky ledge and pull itself up. Then it rotates its hind flippers underneath its body and walks. As a walrus moves onshore, it may prop itself up with its tusks, using them like walking sticks.

Tusks

A walrus's tusks may grow to be more than three feet long. They are mainly used for fighting and getting out of the water.

Whiskers

A walrus uses the whiskers on its snout to feel for food on the sea floor.

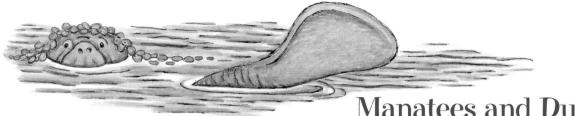

Manatees and Dugongs

Mermaids

Sometimes a dugong or manatee rests onshore. If you use your imagination, it looks a little like a woman with a fish's tail. Maybe that's why sailors once thought they were mermaids.

Manatees and dugongs are warm-water swimmers. Their hairless bodies have only a thin layer of blubber under the skin. This layer is less than one inch thick. These slow-swimming animals cannot stand water that is colder than sixty degrees Fahrenheit.

When a manatee or dugong swims, it flaps its tail and steers with its tail and flippers. It can be surprisingly agile in the water. It can roll, glide on its back, somersault, and even stand on its head. It can stay underwater for up to twenty minutes, but usually comes up for air every two to four minutes.

Manatees and dugongs are sometimes called sea cows. These gentle animals eat sea grasses, leaves, and other plants by using their large, flexible upper lips to guide food to their mouths. They chew the food with flat molar teeth.

manatees

24

Manatee | **Dugong**

round body ● slim body

rounded tail ● forked tail

uses front flippers ● tucks flippers to side
to grab food when swimming

no tusks ● small tusks inside mouth

lives in warm, shallow water ● lives in coastal regions of the
along the east coasts of Indian and Pacific oceans
North and South America

Sea Otters

Sea otters live along the Pacific coast of North America from Alaska to Mexico. A sea otter spends much of its life floating on its back in the water. It swims by paddling with its webbed back feet and steering with its long, rudderlike tail. To move quickly, the otter flips over onto its stomach and propels itself forward, using its feet and an up-and-down motion of its long body.

Sea otters are good divers. A sea otter can stay underwater for up to five minutes as it searches for sea urchins and other food. It returns to the surface to eat and uses its belly as a table. Sea otters can even sleep in the water, draping themselves in kelp to keep from drifting.

Fine Fur Coats

A sea otter does not have thick blubber like most other marine mammals. Instead, it relies on a dense fur coat to keep itself warm. This coat is made of two layers—an outer layer of coarse guard hairs and a thick inner layer of extremely fine hair. The underfur of a sea otter can have up to a million hairs per square inch. Tiny air bubbles trapped in the oily fibers insulate the sea otter's skin and keep it from getting wet. They also help the sea otter to float.

guard hairs

air bubble

underfur

skin

Ringed Seal

Ringed seals are the main prey of polar bears.

Polar Bears

Polar bears live in the Arctic. These fierce predators hunt for seals and other marine mammals on the ice and in the ocean. Polar bears are strong swimmers and can travel sixty miles or more in open water. When swimming, a polar bear holds its head above water and paddles with its large, partially webbed front feet. Thick fur and a layer of fat keep it warm in the icy water. As it swims, it may keep an eye out for seals resting near the water's edge.

In winter most of the open water freezes over. Then polar bears prowl the ice looking for holes where seals come up to breathe. When a seal appears, a polar bear can kill it with one swipe of a powerful front paw.

beaver

Swimming in Freshwater
Beavers, river otters, muskrats, capybaras, and platypuses are some other mammals whose bodies are adapted for swimming. These smaller animals live in freshwater rivers and lakes.

river otters

muskrat

platypus

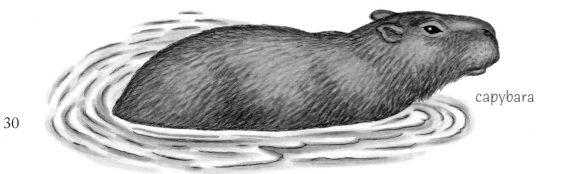

capybara

Super Swimmers

Marine mammals are found in oceans all over the world, from icy polar waters to warm tropical lagoons. You can sometimes see seals and sea lions on the beach or when they are swimming close to shore. If you go out in a boat, you might catch a glimpse of a whale or dolphin swimming alongside. You can also observe marine mammals up close at a zoo or aquarium. You can watch how the animals swim, dive, and move in the water with amazing ease. From acrobatic sea lions and lumbering walruses to playful porpoises and mermaidlike manatees, they are all experts in the water. All the marine mammals have special features that make them supremely suited to life in the sea. They are truly nature's super swimmers.

Glossary

baleen fringed, horny plates that hang from the upper jaw of baleen whales and are used to filter food

blowhole the hole in the top of the head through which a whale, dolphin, or porpoise breathes·

blubber the thick layer of fat between the skin and muscle layers of whales and other marine mammals

breaching when a whale or dolphin jumps partially or completely out of the water

dorsal fin the fin on the back of most whales and dolphins

drag the slowing force of water on a moving object

echolocation a way of locating objects through the use of echoes

flukes the two broad, flat lobes on the tail of a whale, dolphin, or porpoise

keratin the hard material in whale baleen and human fingernails

lobtailing when a whale or dolphin raises its flukes and slaps the water's surface

mammal an animal that gives birth to live young and feeds its babies milk

parasites organisms that live on or in another organism

pectoral flippers the flippers near the front of a whale or dolphin

porpoising when an animal leaps and dives while swimming forward

slipstream the area of reduced pressure or forward suction produced by and immediately behind an object moving quickly through air or water

spyhopping when a whale, dolphin, or porpoise raises its head almost vertically out of the water